DYING

A Guide to a More Peaceful Death

Cynthia Casoff Henry

ISBN: 1482677407
ISBN-13: 9781482677409
Library of Congress Control Number: 2013904175
CreateSpace Independent Publishing Platform
North Charleston, South Carolina

Contents

Dedication

This book is dedicated to those who died yesterday, those who die today, and those who will die tomorrow. And also to those left behind.

Acknowledgments

I want to thank all the patients and their families, who taught me about death and dying, grief and anger, denial and acceptance. I was honored to take part in these intimate times in their lives.

I also want to thank my mother, who I took care of for five and a half years. I lay next to her as she took her final breath.

I thank my husband John for his comfort, support, and patience listening to all my stories.

I am so grateful to Hyacinth Mellad, who taught me so much, as we took care of my mother together at home.

I want to give special thanks and gratitude to Hospice Care of the Berkshires in Massachusetts and Hospice by the Sea in Florida, where I was taught lovingly how to care for patients and families and given the tools and the knowledge for comfort care.

I want to also thank Jill Davis, my niece and editor. With her help, I made this book clearer and easier to read and understand, which is not an easy task with such a powerful subject.

Thanks also to Ivan Anderson for making my words mean what I meant and for making sure my grammar was correct, and a special thanks to the gang at Create Space for holding my hand through the process of publication.

Last but not least, to my family and friends--Barbara Davis, Ellen Lederman, Annette Schickman, Cecile Moochnek, Maryann Arcoleo Koltun, Nikki Brierton, Marcia Spence Glicksman, Richard Werber, Maggie Lapierre, Marilyn Jaffe Ruiz, Maureen Bamberger, and Shirley Mesa. Many thanks for your love and support.

Introduction

What is this book about? What will you, the reader, learn? I hope to help prepare the reader for the end of life—whether the patient is you or your loved one. In this book, I will explain step-by-step how to accomplish a calmer, more accepting end-of-life experience.

As a hospice nurse, I hope to lead you down the path to the end of life with tangible information and also give you true-life examples from my own experiences. I hope to ease you through the many phases. This highly emotional time is often the most difficult cycle of life because of its finality. Travel with me on the journey toward a good death.

This book is for any person who has a very serious illness with a poor prognosis or any person whose loved one has received a devastating diagnosis. This is a book to share with loved ones.

Death is something you only do one time. It's really important to get it as right as you can. And don't forget to give lots of hugs and kisses to those you love as often as possible.

CHAPTER ONE

First Things First

It's best to take care of your living will, funeral arrangements, and general wishes before you get a devastating diagnosis. Having your wishes written down is very important for you as a patient and also for your loved ones. It is always easier to make plans before you get a diagnosis because you are not as anxious—it's not yet real. You can think more clearly. Maybe you've gone online and printed out a living will. You may have taken care of your legal matters with your lawyer. Perhaps you've already changed your health-care surrogate and your personal wishes as you've matured.

In all cases, it's crucial to understand that death comes to all of us and that it is best to be prepared. As we get older, there is a greater likelihood of illness, so it is important to have your advance directives in place. This book is to help guide you through your experience—it's to help you to find your voice for telling your family, friends, doctors, and nurses what you want.

Advance Directives include:

1. Living will: This is where you decide who should make decisions for you if you cannot. It is also a description of what, if any,

life-prolonging medical care you want provided, withheld, or withdrawn if you cannot make your own decisions. This is a decision that you will want someone to respect and follow if you can't speak for yourself and you have a terminal illness, or if you are in a persistent vegetative state.

2. The Five Wishes: This is another form of a living will. It is a document that is written very simply, and it's easy to fill out. Just specify the following:

► who you want to make health-care decisions when you can't make them

► the kind of medical treatment you want or don't want

► how comfortable you want to be

► how you want people to treat you

▶ what you want your loved ones to know

This is not recognized in every state, but it meets legal requirements in most states and is useful in all states. You can check the Internet for which states accept it.

3. Health-care surrogate (HCS): This is the person or persons who will represent you when you can no longer make decisions for yourself. You can also choose an alternate HCS in case the first person is not available. Make sure that whoever you choose agrees with and respects your decisions.

4. Anatomical gifts: This is a written form that indicates your wishes to donate all or part of your body. Make sure the arrangements

are in place and that the health-care surrogate is aware of the process used to carry this out. Often a medical school or teaching hospital will be involved. The form can be easily found on the internet or done on your driver's license.

5. DNRO, or Do Not Resuscitate Order: This would identify that you do not want to be revived in any circumstance. You can get a form from your doctor, from the Department of Health, or from an attorney. If an ambulance is called, and you do not have this form in plain sight, The Emergency Medical Technicians (EMTs) will resuscitate you, even if it's not what you want. Make sure whoever lives with you knows where your DNR form is. And if you live

alone, leave it taped on the refrigerator. The EMTs will look there.

6. POA (Power of Attorney): This is a form that designates and authorizes a person or persons to take care of your financial, legal, and possibly medical issues.

7. Will: This is the document that states what you want to leave to your children, friends, family, and organizations. This can be done by a lawyer, or you can print up forms from the Internet. Make sure that you have a file where this can be found, and that the person you have chosen to represent you has a copy. Make sure that person agrees to respect your wishes.

It is extremely important that you choose a person (or persons) to represent you who will stick with what you've requested. As a hospice nurse, I cannot count how many times I have seen families refuse to do what is specified in the living will. I have seen these families ask for feeding tubes, intravenous drips, tracheotomies, and ventilators (to keep a person breathing). Then I would read the person's living will, which had requested none of the above. When I would ask a family member or HCS why all these medical interventions were ordered, I most often got one of two answers: the most common was "I just can't let go!" The second was "I don't think he/she really meant this!" You must pick a person that will know, trust, and respect that this truly is your desire. The person must understand the importance of carrying out your wishes.

Sometimes it's better to pick someone outside the family—a friend or a lawyer—to represent you. This can be handled by explaining that you don't want to burden the family in time of grief. This truly is your contract for your end of life.

Notes:

CHAPTER TWO

Get the Truth

I know a woman who has been battling brain cancer for the past year. She has had aggressive chemotherapy and radiation. Recently, after having had another brain scan, she got an e-mail from her doctor proposing a plan for more chemotherapy. At the end of the e-mail, the doctor mentioned how sorry he was that new lesions had appeared on the scan. A close friend of this woman mentioned how "nice" the doctor was for expressing his concern. My reaction as a hospice nurse was very different. I wanted to know what else the doctor knew. Had he given his patient all the information she'd need to make a thoughtful, educated decision about her treatment?

After a devastating diagnosis, it is so important to continually get as much truth as possible. Doctors want to cure. They want to do miracles, and sometimes that may happen—but most often it does not. Doctors have begun to get training in end-of-life issues, but it's only a beginning. Promises are often unrealistic. Doctors themselves, including many oncologists, refuse to accept the inevitable until death is imminent. Fight for as much truth as you can get. That way, the last months—even up to a year—can be used in the best possible way.

It is extremely important to get a second opinion after getting a devastating diagnosis. Always bring someone with you to the doctor's office—someone who can listen along with you to what is going on. Those first few visits can be a blur. It's difficult to listen and hear with so much fear and anxiety.

Before going to the doctor, write down your questions. You can get much information online—both questions and answers. It is extremely important to know that the doctor is there for you, and not the other way around. It is truly about *you*. The person you bring with you needs to be strong, preferably with a medical background. If you are not happy with your visits, then you should consider finding another doctor. This is *your* time, and as stressful as it feels, you need to feel that you can control some of the issues. The diagnosis does not need to be cancer for it to be considered life threatening. No matter what the diagnosis is, you need to feel comfortable with your care. When you get your second opinion, the doctor should be affiliated with a different hospital than the one that offered the first opinion. I have known people who even got a third opinion and made their decisions only when two of the three doctors agreed on a plan.

If you find that your family or friends are too stressed, too frightened to be of any help, there are health-care advocates for hire. There is a range of prices from state to state. You can also contact a hospice in your area, and they can suggest a palliative-care group.

Hospice care focuses on bringing comfort, tranquility, and self-respect to the dying patient and family. Control of patient symptoms—which may be physical, spiritual, emotional, or social pain—helps the dying patient face the end of life, giving comfort and quality of life. Usually the patient is diagnosed with six or fewer months to live.

Palliative care is an area of health care that focuses on relieving and preventing suffering of patients in all disease phases.

Both hospice and palliative care utilize a team approach, which includes physicians, nurses, social workers, psychologists, and those who provide spiritual care.

Part of getting the truth is getting to understand how much time you have and what the quality of your life looks like—with treatment and without. The illness does not need to be cancer. It could be heart disease, Alzheimer's, Parkinson's, COPD (Chronic Obstructive Pulmonary Disease), or ALS, for example. Getting to the truth about timing is extraordinarily difficult to do but necessary. Most doctors can give you a ballpark figure—never exact. A precise timeline comes at the very, very end stage, when both doctor and family can often tell that the patient has only days, or even hours, left.

As a hospice nurse, I have seen so many people getting aggressive treatment when both the diagnosis and the appearance of the patient showed me that it was too late. Doctors want to give patients hope, but there are times when the hope is gone and it is time to accept and be at peace. This of course is very, very difficult. Not only does the patient need to hear and accept the truth, but family and loved ones need to hear and accept it, too. There are patients who cannot and will not face the truth, so the burden for their care and end-of-life choices falls to family, friends, or partners. This is a big burden.

This moment is so emotionally charged— everyone involved needs to step away and think about what is best for the patient. I believe the truth sets us free. Though getting there is an enormous challenge, it should be the main goal for an advocate. Many doctors are put off, even annoyed—whether you are a friend or family member—at being questioned, but it is your right and an obligation to the patient.

Important questions to ask and how to ask them

If you are a patient, you can ask a doctor yourself, or have your health-care surrogate ask. It is important not to be aggressive, but to have the doctor in a comfortable place to explain and not feel threatened:

1. Doctor, how am I doing? How will the treatment affect me? And what can I expect?

2. What can I expect after treatment? Will I be very tired, or sick, and how long does it take for the chemo and radiation side effects to wear off?

3. Doctor, how long do you think I have? I realize this is such a difficult question,

but do you have an idea so I can make plans?

4. Do you think that the treatments will eventually lengthen my life and give me a better quality?

5. What can I do to make a difference, besides chemo and radiation? (Meaning diet, supplements, anything else.)

6. Doctor, can you tell me when there comes a time when treatment won't makes sense for me, and can you help me get to the best place for me for the end of life?

7. Doctor, I so appreciate your expertise at such a difficult time, and I would so appreciate your keeping me informed about my progress and how my disease is either progressing or regressing. I want to be realistic.

To repeat: the above questions can also be used by the health-care surrogate if the patient is unable to ask because of disease or anxiety. Try not to ask too many questions at one visit. But do write down your questions in preparation.

Getting the truth is the beginning of the journey toward a peaceful death. Once you know the truth, there is help in planning for the end of life for a loved one. Hospice and palliative care will help you, but grief counselors are helpful as well, since not only is the diagnosis devastating to the patient but to loved ones. People need to come together to make this the most meaningful and least painful experience possible.

Once you know the truth, it's absolutely okay—and necessary, in fact—to take the time you need to grieve. Give yourself permission to mourn the life you thought you would have—to miss the time you thought you had left, the people you love, the places you enjoy. In order to move on to the next phase, you might consider medication for depression, and you might consider psychotherapy. Therapy and mood stabilizers can help you cope and help you manage the future you have left. A good therapist can help you organize your plans. None of this is easy—it is a very complex journey, and no doubt you will need support in order to cope with the questions and reactions of loved ones. Try to remember that your goal is to get to a place of peace for the end of life.

It will feel like an overwhelming responsibility, but facing the truth (and your feelings about the truth) and making necessary plans will make you feel free. And soon you will begin to accept your final destination.

Notes:

CHAPTER THREE

Get a Plan Together

After you have gotten a second opinion or even a third, and if two doctors agree, pick the doctor you feel the most comfortable with. Together you should work out a plan. Remember to bring someone with you to all visits to help you. Bringing a friend or relative helps you keep up with progress reports—by taking notes, listening closely, or asking questions. Never feel that you or your companion is bothering the doctor. This is your life and your experience. The doctor is there for you—even if it doesn't always seem that way.

At the same time you begin traditional treatment, you and your family or advocate might look into alternative treatment. This may include acupuncture, yoga, meditation, nutritional counsel, and herbal remedies. Make sure to look up any herbal remedies you take. Sometimes herbal remedies and traditional medications react with each other, causing unpleasant side effects. Write down questions and keep a list with you. Always ask about what to expect: What side effects are likely? What can I do to be prepared for these side effects?

Be kind to yourself at this time. Schedule some relaxing activities, such as massages, manicures, pedicures, hair appointments, and lunches with friends. If you are going to get chemotherapy (cancer medication by mouth or IV) that will make you lose your hair, you will need to decide if you want to cover your head. Most people use wigs, scarves, or hats. If you need surgery for breast cancer, you may lose a breast or both breasts. You will need to think about whether you want reconstruction surgery or special bras made for mastectomy. Whatever the treatment, you will need to know what to expect and to plan ahead in order to make life more comfortable with your situation.

For some diseases, an ostomy is necessary. This is a hole inside your body surgically created for the discharge of body wastes. Some people require colostomy (colon/large intestine), ileostomy (ileum/small intestine), tracheostomy (trachea), or others. These treatments may also come with a sense of loss. Take time to grieve. You are losing a body function, and you need time to adjust. Give yourself time and permission to grieve, and allow your partner to feel his or her feelings. None of this comes easily. It is a struggle. I strongly urge you to seek outside help from social workers, psychologists, and psychiatrists who are out there to help you.

There are times when antidepressants are a good idea. Getting a devastating diagnosis can often cause depression or emotional paralysis. In order to function and move forward during your treatment, both physically and emotionally, it might serve you, the patient, to get some help.

Family Cooperation

Once you have decided on your treatment plan and have discussed the plan with your family and friends, it is important for you to know that everyone is on board and in agreement with the decisions you've made with your doctors. Conflict causes so much stress. As a hospice nurse, I have seen many families split apart over treatment plans. I have seen family members who want only alternative therapy while the other members want only traditional therapies. In these situations, someone can and should help bridge the gap. It is too burdensome for the patient to try to please everyone. The patient's energy must go into coping with treatments, not family arguments. Compromise is the best way to go—even if it's an outside party, a mediator is often needed to help manage the decision making.

Illness is not necessarily a logical situation. Nor is it predictable. Sometimes people get better and other times not. Sometimes the treatments—especially chemotherapy—cause a big decline. There needs to be flexibility in the care plan. Sometimes the treatment needs to stop temporarily, depending on the reaction the patient has. Sometimes it needs to be stopped permanently. I have seen many patients say, "Enough! No more!" Families and doctors need to respect this decision depending on the situation. The plan can change to include switching to hospice or palliative care. It depends how far the disease has progressed. We will discuss this in Chapter Six.

Reader, if you have not made personal plans, this would be a good time to do it. Put your papers in order. This is a time when you can still feel in charge. You can plan things to be done the way you want them. Choose a helper who will actually respect your wishes instead of trying to convince you to do what you don't want.

Notes:

CHAPTER FOUR

When to Stop Traditional Treatment

The most important part of determining whether to stop treatment comes from looking at the quality of life of the patient. The first step is getting good information on the progression of the disease. The patient, family, or health-care surrogate can obtain this information.

Listening to the patient is of prime importance. So many times in my experience, the patient will say, "No more," but loved ones have such difficulty with this and put a great deal of pressure on the patient to continue treatment.

There have been times in my work when patients have begged me to tell the family "No more." Sometimes I have done this and found that the family is able to listen and really hear it, but for more resistant families I have asked the doctor to sit with the family and explain that death is near and that even if medical intervention is used, it will cause more discomfort and possibly only give a couple more days with little quality of life.

As a hospice nurse, I saw patients' loved ones in pain and anguish. They were not sleeping, eating, or able to cope—unable to accept the inevitable, the loss. This was the most difficult yet most rewarding part of my work. It was gratifying to be able to help families, loved ones, and most of all, to help the patient reach the point of acceptance. Once they could accept the inevitable and let go of the idea of getting better, they moved on, finally living the last part of their lives with the benefit of comfort measures. Each person needs to come to some form of acceptance. Though helping people understand this idea is a colossal undertaking, it can be done and is done every day. This can be a very freeing time. In my experience, it can be a calming time for family and loved ones.

When a patient's behavior, pain level, or agitation increases, or when the patient has severe respiratory issues, this often signals the end of life. At this point, we should treat symptoms with comfort measures. Besides pain medication, there is music therapy, healing touch, massage, and pet therapy—which are all important for comfort. Comfort measures are a gift. They allow the person to accept the inevitable with less suffering. Comfort measures are gentle, loving, and soothing for the soul. Because they feel so soothing, they can take people away from the sadness, the sorrow, the sense of loss—even if for a short time.

Studies have shown that for themselves, doctors often request comfort only, with little or no intervention at the end of life. Ken Murray, a journalist for the *Wall Street Journal*, has written an excellent article on the subject titled "Why Doctors Die Differently."

There are always going to be the "what ifs." I have heard patients and family members say,

"What if we stop treatment and there really is help and he or she can live longer?"

When this comes up, it's time to look at the patient's quality of life. When a person is admitted to a hospice, the patient's doctor and the hospice doctor agree that the patient only has six months or fewer to live. Again, that means the patient's disease process is very advanced. I have seen families remove the patient from hospice care to seek something more aggressive, and their loved one died within twenty-four hours of leaving the hospice care center. The family could not accept that death was near.

I remember working with the son of a patient who was near death. The patient was a woman who'd already had several surgeries for colon cancer. Her son believed—against my advice—that she'd benefit from yet more. On his own, he called the surgeon, and the surgeon agreed to take his mother into the operating room for an additional surgery. She was removed from hospice care and transferred to the ICU, but by the time the surgeon got to the ICU the next morning, the patient had died.

Soon after she died, the woman's son came to see us in the hospice unit. He was able to tell us then that he realized he simply hadn't been able to hear what we were trying to tell him, that he was sad that he hadn't been able to accept the truth. We understood. We were able to find a grieving group, and there he was able to work out a lot of these feelings of regret.

There is a great deal of mistrust toward the medical profession. This is an age-old issue that medical professionals understand, however, and hospice doctors, nurses, and social workers are very well trained with end-of-life care and have an exhaustive understanding of the dying process.

This topic also becomes very complicated when a physician can't let go. This is why it is so important to have deep conversations with your doctors beforehand, so that you understand the doctors' approach to death when the disease process has progressed so far and there is very little quality to life and no miracle cures. Families and patients sometimes need to help the doctor and say to him or her, "Enough. No more." You need to know that your doctor will respect your wishes, also. Medicine is not an exact science, especially at the end of life. Death is not a failure; it is simply the end part of life.

Notes:

CHAPTER FIVE

Discuss Your Death and Wishes

A woman came on to the hospice unit in poor shape. She was very clear with me—she knew she was dying. As I admitted her, she told me that her family, including her two adult children and four grandchildren, was having a hard time accepting that nothing else could be done for her. Her chart indicated that she had a living will, but that it had been written years ago. I asked her if she had spoken recently to her family about her wishes. Her answer was no, she hadn't.

I offered to stay with her while she spoke to her family about what she felt happening to her body and what her wishes were. She thought about it for a while and decided that yes, it would be a good idea if I stayed. She telephoned her two children and invited them to visit and bring their children. They arrived two hours later, and it was easy to see how anxious they all felt. There had been no realistic communication between them up to this point.

I stood quietly by the patient's side as she sat herself up in the bed. She was weak. She was tired. But she summoned up the strength to tell her loved ones that she was going to die soon.

She told them that she was at peace, and that she loved them all. But she told them she had to go. Everyone there (including the writer) was teary eyed and full of emotion. Their initial reaction was to say, "Not yet! Not yet!" But the patient was clear. What was coming was now out of her control, and the end was near. She could feel it. They were extremely upset and angry, so I decided to take the family out of the room. The patient was weak and exhausted. I followed the family out and listened. They struggled with wanting to do more. "Why *couldn't* she get better?" they asked. We talked and talked, and I explained, "You have to let her go. She knows what her body is going through."

It took a good long while, but eventually they were able to hear me. It was her wish to be at peace. She knew that her disease had taken hold. And now they had to let her go. This would be their gift to her. They stayed with her for the day, and before my shift ended each family member had told her they loved her and that it was okay for her to go.

When I came back to work the next morning, she had died. It had happened during the night, and the family had stayed to be with her. The night staff said that the family was very sad, but accepting.

It doesn't often go this well, but this type of positive outcome is the goal—that is, to be able to openly discuss your death, your final wishes, and to feel your family's acceptance and respect. We don't have to wait until the end. Families can address the many various issues anytime.

When you've written your will and your living will, it's also a good opportunity to share your feelings with your family and friends. Another excellent opportunity is at the time the illness is diagnosed. Once the initial shock wears off, it's a good time to have a family discussion. Don't forget to review your plans with your physician, who is also your representative.

Too many times I have heard people, including my own family members, say, "I'm not ready to talk about it." I always answer back, "It will never be easy, but if you can talk about it at a time that's non-urgent, and not a crisis, your wishes and desires will come across calmer, clearer, and more convincingly." Now is your chance to be clear to everyone involved. After all, your other goal is to remove any feeling of burden from those you love, those who will have to to make these decisions for you if you don't do it first.

And you should discuss your funeral if you have strong feelings about what you want. Maybe you know already that you want a traditional funeral. Or maybe you prefer a very quiet small funeral or memorial later on. Is there a specific song or type of music you want played? You can write your own obituary. Many people who have done this tell me they feel like they are truly part of the experience. It is yours to do if you want to.

On the other hand, there are many examples of families or patients not being able to discuss their death. This, of course, causes much turmoil and emotional discomfort within families. Hospice staff work very hard to achieve a peaceful end of life, but there is often great resistance.

This comes out in many ways because these people are in denial of the inevitable. I have witnessed this conflict so many times. The most common form of denial is when the end of life is close, and either a nurse or social worker will try to discuss funeral arrangements—and family members refuse to do this. What I have often said is that it's easier to make arrangements now, because after the death there is so much grieving that it's difficult to make phone calls for arrangements; even so, there are a great number of people who simply cannot discuss the funeral at this point.

There is also a group of people who don't want their loved ones to know they are dying. Sometimes patients actually know they are dying, but also know that the family doesn't want them to know. And other times, the patient really doesn't know. But of these situations, it is most difficult for the patients who know they are dying but are not able to talk it through with loved ones. It burdens the patient. Hopefully, the patient is in a hospice setting and can get comfort from staff.

One patient who didn't know she was dying was terribly frightened and felt lost because there was never a sense of peace or acceptance about the end of life—not with herself nor with her family. The family didn't want her to know.

These examples illustrate how difficult and harmful it can be if we don't communicate these powerful decisions and needs. But you can change that, and it can be a peaceful, more accepting experience for everyone.

Notes:

CHAPTER SIX

Hospice and Palliative Care

When touring families for the Hospice Care Center Unit, I've found so many families in conflict about their loved one. So many of these family members are unable to accept giving up aggressive treatments even though they've been told nothing more can be done. This usually means the disease has progressed too far for treatment to help.

This is when it's time to discuss hospice and palliative care. Hospice care is generally for people who have six months or fewer to live. Palliative care is performed by doctors, nurses or nurse practitioners, social workers, spiritual-care providers, and others whose job it is to help people transition down from aggressive treatment. They help by making suggestions to other physicians on how to help the patient—this includes symptomatic care, such as pain control, calming of severe agitation, and relief of extreme nausea and vomiting. In my experience, I have found that physicians and nurses are afraid of morphine and other narcotics. There is a stigma about using large doses of narcotics. Hospice and palliative-care staff are not afraid to use what is necessary. They are very creative and know how to use narcotics to control the most uncomfortable symptoms. I've seen tiny, frail women and men into their nineties being given very large doses of narcotics to control pain for long periods of time. They are actually better because the medicine controls their pain. More education about useful narcotics would help all of us—families, patients, doctors, nurses, and the public in general. Neither hospice nor palliative care heals the patient. Both are strictly meant to provide comfort. What is your family member ready for? I have met many families who were not ready for comfort care—this is where palliative care is a wonderful step. The patient can still get intravenous and other more aggressive treatments but still have an experienced team, watching and supervising proper comfort care.

When the palliative care group suggests hospice care, the family comes face to face with the reality—that the end is inevitable. They may need help coping emotionally. Both groups of people, palliative and hospice staff, work very hard to guide patients and their loved ones toward a more peaceful, calmer experience—the goal being less chaos, less anger, more acceptance, more peace, and much more comfort for the person who is dying. I would often ask, "What would you want?" to the family member still pushing for aggressive treatment. Palliative and hospice staff aim to lessen the fear and anger associated with death and dying, and they feel great satisfaction when people come together and a peaceful death occurs.

So when is the right time for hospice care? This is an important decision. Knowing where the patient and family want to be for hospice care is the next question. There are many choices. There are assisted living facilities (ALFs), skilled nursing facilities, or home.

In an ALF, the patient has to be able to do most self-care on his own with some assistance from the ALF. Hospice staff can oversee care—providing knowledge and guidance to the staff of the facility—but they don't stay there. The family can hire private aides to help with daily care, which can be costly.

In skilled nursing facilities, there is twenty-four-hour nursing care available, but often the patients do not get the attention they need. Hospice staff oversee care but do not offer personal one-on-one care for large blocks of time.

Then there is home. This is what most people want and is probably the most complicated option. Families learn quickly how difficult and involved it is to take care of a loved one at home. It is all consuming. Your life, no longer your own, revolves around the patient's issues, including administering medications, doctor visits, and any personal needs, such as bathing and toileting. Your loved one feels content, but inevitably it will be exhausting, frustrating, and sometimes scary.

Hospice staff supervise home care, and some fortunate families can hire private help. Families should know that most hospices offer a five-day respite care one time a month. Families get a break from the grueling daily routine of complete care. Many people want their loved one to die at home. Some people want their loved one to go to a hospice care center for the last few days or hours. They are afraid to have death in their home. I took care of my own mother at home for five and a half years—and she died at home. For me, it was a very special experience. I knew it was what she wanted, and my many years of hospice training helped enormously. I was also able to have help at home, which made a big difference. If families can make it work, being at home is best because the patient is surrounded with her own sounds and smells, and life remains familiar, and that is a comfort.

There are also hospice houses around the country that will allow people to live their last weeks, and sometimes months, there. These are few and far between. Each state has its own rules and regulations for what is legal and safe, however, with budget cuts to Medicare, Medicaid, and other medical insurance companies, the period of time a patient is allowed to stay on in hospice may be shortened. If so, the patient can often move into a different setting, such as a home setting, an assisted living setting, or a skilled nursing facility.

There is so much fear still attached to death and dying. Hospice workers try very hard to work with people at all levels of fear and concern. Whichever way people choose or however the choice is made, hospice and palliative care are available to everyone and serve as invaluable ways to help families with their loved ones' illness and death. Hospice care centers administer grievance groups as well. These are available free of charge for one year after the death of a loved one, even if the person that died was not on hospice care.

Notes:

CHAPTER SEVEN

Review Your Life

I worked in hospice care in Massachusetts with a social worker that showed patients how to do what was called a life review—in this case it was an album with pictures and words. Taking time to put words and images together, focusing on peak moments with family members, was not only therapeutic for the patient but for the family also. Not all hospices do this automatically, but it is a tool that many patients can use on their own or with help from a family member.

What exactly is a life review? It can mean different things. It can mean sitting with a loved one and talking about his life—which can go back to childhood and grade school up through all education and early experiences, then on to marriage, children, grandchildren. You can even record this or someone can write it down for you. Photo albums are also a wonderful way to look back.

A good friend of mine was divorced and started to date a new man. She put together an album of her adventures from her own childhood to the present day and showed him what her life had looked like. This can be done so that the person at the end of life can see what his own life looked like. It will also be a precious keep-sake for loved ones.

Life review can also include written or verbal situations that aren't as pleasant. It's always wonderful to find yourself in a place with few regrets, but most people aren't so lucky. As you are preparing life review, you will need to include people you have stopped talking to for various reasons. Upon looking back, you often realize that in the end, the reason for the split wasn't very important—perhaps it was a family squabble or a silly comment blown out of proportion.

With e-mail, Facebook, and other simple ways to communicate, there are great ways to recon-nect without a face-to-face meeting. If you are not able to communicate this way, you can get a grandchild or a friend to help you. I have seen a lot of people reconnect and let go of old feuds—which, at this time of life, seem senseless. These are unresolved issues that can lead to a freer you.

Talk to social workers, spiritual leaders, or others if you need help. On the other hand, if you have an estranged relative who is dying and you want to connect, please do so. Call, send a letter, pay a visit. You can say, "I'm sorry, and I love you. Let's let bygones be bygones, enjoy one another, and remember the important times we had together." There is no need to rehash in detail, unless you really feel it will help you heal.

What can be very difficult is knowing how to talk to a dying person who is either minimally responsive or not responsive at all. When my own mother had a massive stroke, she became unresponsive. I called my sisters and told them to come. A while later, my niece and nephew each called on the phone. Holding the receiver up to my mother's ear, each one spoke to her, telling her they loved her. She could no longer speak, but I could see by her facial expression that she heard them. Soon most of the family was there, and that's when she died.

Speaking to a person who cannot respond is difficult. It's almost like speaking to yourself. I would often tell families to talk as though they were getting a response. Hearing is the last sense to go before a person dies. Think of what you would want to hear if you were dying—use loving words, soft touches. Here are some examples: "You were a great mom." "You were the perfect dad." "Thank you for all the help, knowledge, and kindness." "I remember so many great times together." These loving and affectionate words, along with gentle touching, help loved ones die peacefully. It can be an elating experience for you.

It is so important to consider the many aspects of a person's life, especially if she can no longer ask for what she needs. While sitting at the bedside of a person who is not conscious, family members and friends can do so much: keeping company, holding hands, and talking. Often as a hospice nurse, I saw the patient's eye movements even though the eyes were closed. What a wonderful gift! Loved ones can and should put the patient first—even though it's a challenging task. It takes a great deal of strength and love to put someone else's needs first.

Death feels very scary, but it is important to go beyond your own fears to help the person on his last stop. Death will come to us all. I have often spoken with loved ones, and, in many cases, I even helped them look to the future and think about how they themselves want to die— as hard as that sounds.

We should all review our lives every so often. We should do it a little at a time, rather than wait until we are dying. Take the time. Tell the people you are close with that you love them. Cherish your moments together. I cannot tell you how often I've heard "I didn't tell him/her often enough how much I appreciated/loved/respected/ admired him." Do this while this person is alive and aware—and if you haven't yet, you can still do it. The patient is still present even if he is not able to talk. The patient can still hear you.

Review your life along the way.

Notes:

CHAPTER EIGHT

End-of-Life-Symptoms

How does one know when it's close to the end of life? The average person depends on the medical community for this kind of help and information.

Generally a person close to the end of life becomes less responsive or appears to be sleeping more (or most) of the time. She will have very little desire to eat. She may not be able to eat at all. This person may be in extreme pain, and this includes emotional pain. People can also exhibit nausea and vomiting. Breathing patterns can change, becoming slower and more labored.

The medical and emotional needs of this person increase now, as do the needs of the patient's caregivers. It is so important to have a good support system of family and friends—and also a good medical support system to help you through these symptoms.

Pain can be physical or emotional. Both kinds of pain can be treated with medications. For physical pain, there are many medications available—both narcotic and not. The biggest hurdle is addressing the patient's family, who often fear that the patient will become addicted to the narcotic. The staff at a hospice know how to manage pain control very effectively. The medicine goes to the pain centers and works on the pain. Too many times I have seen a patient cry out because a relative felt he wasn't awake enough to take the narcotic. I've asked this relative, "Why would you want your loved one to feel this way? What would you want for yourself?"

It is a hard concept for family members to understand, but eventually we hope they'll get to a place where they can say, "Yes, comfort first."

I once worked with a patient's daughter. The patient herself was in extreme pain. Being a nurse, the daughter knew a lot and felt she needed to control her mother's intake of narcotics. One day, her mother was calling out in excruciating pain, but the daughter refused pain medication. Finally, I asked her to come to her mother's room and told her that she needed to see that her mother was suffering—that this was not about her, but about her mother's comfort. I got permission from her to give her mother the proper dose of medication, and soon the mother was much more peaceful. In turn, the daughter felt unburdened knowing her mother was in less pain.

Nausea and vomiting are also extremely debilitating. Medicines are available to help: crackers, ginger ale, ice chips, and flat Coca-Cola—whatever the person can tolerate.

Another important way to control pain is with massage therapy, healing touch, and music therapy. I have seen many people in enormous discomfort be able to sing along with their old favorite songs with a music therapist. It takes them to a wonderful place with great memories. These adjunct therapies can give a great sense of relief and relaxation. Human touch and attention are extremely important to dying people. Families generally respond very well to seeing this.

All the adjunct therapies help enormously with end of life agitation—along with medications that are needed. I have found this to be the case over and over again. So many patients who get end-of-life diagnoses become depressed and do need anti-anxiety medications or anti-depressants—but I have also found that paying attention to physical touch is just as important.

Family support and education is a large part of helping with any end-of-life symptoms.

Notes:

CHAPTER NINE

Giving Away Your Possessions

I remember one of my sweet lady patients trying to tell her children (three daughters and four sons) what she wanted to leave to each one. As she spoke to them, they said, "But you'll get better, you'll see!" It was too hard for them to hear. They could not accept it. Finally she said, "I'm not getting better, and I need to do this so I will be free of this burden."

Not too many people are this clear and strong. Families have so much difficulty with the end of life of a loved one.

I have also witnessed the opposite—when giving away of possessions is not arranged ahead of time. I've seen family members arguing in front of the patient about what they want, or what they plan to take. This issue splits families up.

During this time—calm or crisis—it is so important to be able to tell people what they will get or what they will inherit. Sometimes there is no will. Having a will that lists your possessions and who you want to have them is an important and very good thing to do. If there is no will, it's best to tell people what you want them to have.

Shortly after getting a poor prognosis people will start giving away their possessions—

especially those with sentimental meaning, such as jewelry and art. Sometimes they just give money. Many people prefer to see their loved ones enjoying their possessions before they die. Gifts make us happy—it's like a celebration before the end of life.

It's also an unburdening of things, freeing up time for the most important time of your life—so that you can be with your loved ones with as few interruptions and distractions as possible. But possessions can get in the way if the issue isn't settled. As with everything else, this is such a complicated issue. Our possessions and our money get confused, caught up, and mixed in with love, family rivalry, sadness, jealousy, and all of it. If people are not sensitive and aware enough to understand this, it becomes consuming, and they are missing the point—which is to be there for the person who is dying.

Another example of this "displaced stress" was the time I walked into a dying patient's room to find her son and daughter arguing about the furniture their mom had in her home. I asked them to leave the room. Outside I explained to them that their mom could hear them—that this was an issue that should be settled in private.

If there are important possessions that have yet to be assigned to a daughter or son, don't argue about them in front of a dying parent. Instead, have family meetings and discussions, or seek assistance from an outside source. As a hospice nurse, these are some of the saddest times for me. To see people squabbling over "stuff" while their loved one is dying and in need of their loving attention.

How sad it is to get caught up with superficial needs. Your loved one is the only real "jewel." This is another example of what I'd call "It's not about you." And it's not. It's about the person in your life who is very sick and nearing the end. Yes, your emotions will be all over the place. It is difficult in these times of crisis to make sense of it all—but it's paramount to step back and realize what truly is important for this person. Savor the last moments.

Notes:

CHAPTER TEN

This is Your Experience

There is a common thread with the end of life—I have seen it so many times. As the patient declines, families and friends try to control a loved one's experience and leave the patient out of the decision-making. I have actually heard people saying, "We will do chemo, then radiation. We will do this, that, or the other," without having included or even consulted the patient.

These people care deeply for their loved one, but cannot let go at a time when the disease process has advanced too far, even though the doctor has already said that further treatment will not help. Even though the patient may be in a great deal of pain or agitated—even though he or she may have increased nausea and vomiting—he or she should still be involved in making these decisions.

Other end-of-life patients may be over-medicated, also making it difficult to be part of the decision-making process. But whatever your condition is as a patient, this is your experience. This is why it's so important to have picked a person or persons to make your decisions that truly respects and honors your wishes. That person is there to advocate for you even under these difficult circumstances, empowering you, the patient, to make as many of your own decisions as possible.

I remember a patient, a man, who so wanted to let go, but his family had such a difficult time with the idea that he was dying. One day, I walked into his room and saw how much pain he was enduring by trying to be strong. It was so clear to me. I advocated for this man by showing his family how he was struggling to stay alive for them. I told them that they needed to let him go and let him go peacefully. I told the family in the man's presence, and when he heard my words and looked at me with pleading eyes, his family saw the truth for the first time, and they understood.

As a hospice nurse, I have had many patients like this man, who ask me to help. Sometimes I can do this, and other times I need to get the social worker involved. It is a team effort. Sometimes the doctor has to speak openly and honestly with the patient and family about what is realistic.

Whether patients can or cannot actually say it, often they really need to go. And they need to say it. Being able to say, "Enough!" or "No more!" or even "I'm ready!" is taking charge of your own death. When this time comes, you have truly come to terms with the end of life. There is acceptance and a certain sense of relief. This is such a personal and deep experience each person comes to—it's having enough strength to accept the inevitable, and allowing yourself to let go, say good-bye, and arrive wherever your mind takes you. A very private and personal experience, this will be different for everyone.

Notes:

CHAPTER ELEVEN

Food and Nutrition and the End of Life

One day at the hospice care center where I worked, an adorable ninety-six-year-old lady came up to me and said, "What am I going to do with the potato salad?" I asked her what she meant. She explained that her ninety-five-year-old sister was a patient on our unit, and that her daughter had called to say she was going to die very soon. So she went home and immediately made several trays of potato salad for the wake! Her sister didn't die that day or even the next. She died a week later, so now she had to go home and make more potato salad!

No matter what culture you come from, food and nutrition is the most difficult concept for people to understand at the end of life. We all have to eat to live. People look at their loved ones losing weight, or with poor appetite, or not eating at all, and they start to believe they're being "starved to death."

Visitors will bring the patient's favorite food and try to feed it to her, hoping the dish will make the difference. But the patient often refuses food of any kind. Loss of appetite and weight loss is part of the dying process.

In the first stages of a serious diagnosis, it is fine to encourage people to eat and drink, but as the disease progresses, the patient shows little interest and has little need for food. One day at work I admitted a woman who (during the admission process) told me that she knew she was dying soon, but her last wish was to have a full lobster meal. So she did! Her two adult children arranged for an eight-pound lobster—cooked up with all the trimmings—to be sent from the state of Maine right to her room. And she ate just about all of it, loved it, and died one and a half days later!

Not all people can do this, nor do they need to. We see so much information about high protein and high-carbohydrate foods and recipes for people who are sick—but for terminal patients, sometimes a sip of water or some juice is all they can handle. This is very normal for the end of life. But when the patients feel bad because they are being pressured by the family about eating, it can cause problems. They're hearing that if they could only gain weight, they'd get better. Most sick people know this is not true.

The issues of intravenous fluids and tube feedings come up daily. We in hospice care know that at the end of life, any kind of feeding rarely helps a patient gain weight or feel better. It usually causes more discomfort. Some of what happens, particularly with intravenous feeding, is that the patient's body gets swollen and overloaded with fluids because the body can no longer process the fluids properly. Disease makes that even worse. One can have nausea and vomiting and aspiration pneumonia from these feeds, so feeding a dying patient *will cause more harm than good.*

Unfortunately, as a hospice nurse I've had to use that expression many times. The body knows even if the mind doesn't.

Working with families around this issue is so very complicated and difficult. Family members and friends want to help. They don't want to "give up." They are often suspicious of medical people—even hospice staff—who allow patients to discontinue food and fluids. But hospice staff and anyone knowledgeable with end-of-life care are there to help family members understand that being dehydrated can actually decrease gastric secretions, which in turn will decrease nausea and vomiting. In this case, an empty stomach becomes a great comfort measure. Unfortunately, aspiration pneumonia is relatively common with terminal patients whose families continue to feed them, and then you have the added discomfort of having to suction the person who is unable to swallow.

This is a very difficult position for families to be in. Making these decisions about food is very powerful. Hopefully, there is a living will that speaks to this issue, making these decisions easier. But if there is no living will, particularly in large families, this can become a very complicated situation involving impassioned disagreements. This is when finding a person educated in death and dying can be very helpful. There is so much emotion involved, especially when adult children have to make decisions for their parents. Letting go of a loved one is very difficult. It is so important when it comes to food and nutrition to think of the quality of life and the comfort of the sick person.

Many times people will choose to stop eating while they have their faculties. This choice is a strong statement, and needs to be respected. More than anyone else, they know what is going on in their body. This is not a selfish "act." This is a person who knows. It is time to die, and the disease has taken hold. We must respect this person's wish—verbal or not.

Notes:

CHAPTER TWELVE

Sudden Death

Even the most seasoned person, the person that feels so prepared for death and dying, cannot prepare for the sudden death of a loved one. There is no time to prepare. One one goes from zero to one hundred twenty miles per hour instantly. The mind cannot believe that it is real. It is impossible to accept the suddenness of this type of death or loss without experiencing any grief from a period of illness.

My brother-in-law, age seventy, was told he was in good health a month before he left to teach in India. He left Boston with his daughter—my niece—who was going along on the adventure. They went with faculty from Boston University to The American School in Bombay, where they taught for five days—and then planned a five-day holiday exploring Rajasthan, further north. The teaching went well, and on the morning of the fifth day, they flew to the lakeside city of Udaipur.

I was at work, and around 2:12 in the afternoon I checked my cell phone, and there was a message from my niece telling me that her dad was sick. She asked me to call her and give her some suggestions. It took me forty minutes to reach her. I needed permission from the cell-phone service provider; I didn't have an international plan. I finally reached her, and she was very upset. I asked her what was happening, and she said, "Dad is dying."

In the meantime, she had gotten her father by ambulance to a local hospital, and by the time I reached her, my brother-in-law had already "fainted" a few times. By now, my niece said they were sticking needles in his chest and doing CPR. She stood twelve feet from where they worked on him. I told her to go and be with him—and she asked me to call her mom, my sister, whom she had been unable to reach.

I was completely traumatized knowing my brother-in-law was probably gone at this time.

I felt for my niece who had never seen anything like this. I was immediately able to reach my sister who was at a friend's home. (In another few months, they would have celebrated their forty-eighth wedding anniversary.) When my sister heard my voice she knew something was wrong. She knew her daughter had left her a message, but she was unable to reach her in India. I told her she needed to call India. She asked me to tell her what was happening, so I told her that her husband was very sick and it sounded like he was dying. I didn't want to tell her he had died, even though I knew in my heart that he had. My sister listened to everything I said and repeated it to her friend. She was clearly in shock.

For the next two and a half hours I was on the telephone to relatives who were equally shocked.

I eventually heard back from my niece. Her father had died. I spoke with my sister, and of course she was still in shock. Her friend would drive her home, and her son was going to meet her there. My job was to notify family members. Every single person I called had the same reaction of disbelief—as though I were telling them a story that wasn't true. We'd all known my brother-in-law since he was eighteen. How could this have happened?

Here I was, a hospice nurse for eight and a half years, working so closely with death and dying, and this sudden death—so close and personal—took my breath away. At the writing of this book, it is three and a half months since the death of my brother-in-law, and the irony is that today, the day I am writing this chapter, would be his seventy-first birthday. My sister has a tremendous support system—including two very devoted children. Her daughter, who withstood something that few people (other than medical people) see, was smart enough to go for grief counseling. Her son, who was very close with his dad, has very good friends and a close family, as well.

All death is loss, but sudden death is like something being ripped from your heart. Grief counsel from any venue is very helpful: friends, therapists, spiritual or religious groups. A person needs to let time pass to take it all in and accept something so sudden and final.

Hospices offer bereavement groups even if the person wasn't on hospice care. It is a form of community outreach. There are therapists who specialize in grieving. It is very important to allow yourself to feel the loss, the pain, the emptiness. Sudden death or loss never makes sense; there is no sequence, no illness—and then suddenly there is nothing. We have to face that empty space when it hurts—embrace the love, feel the person within yourself. Reach out to people that can help you. Realize that healing takes time. For some it takes longer than for others; there are no rules here.

Notes:

CHAPTER THIRTEEN

Dying

Most people know when death is near, even if they can't tell you verbally. There is a look—an aura—and it's almost always very peaceful. Hopefully, all arrangements have been made; all that needs to be said has been said. More than anything, acceptance of the moment is necessary to experience a peaceful death.

Acceptance is of utmost importance for both the person who is dying and for his loved ones. It can be called acceptance, acknowledgment, tolerance, or recognition. In any case, the moment is here. Acknowledgment takes away fear of the unknown. There is a particular look of peace on the face of a dying person who has accepted death. It is a beatific look.

Patients in this peaceful place who have been able to talk have told me they felt a sense of accomplishment: all had been done, they felt a certain well-being, and they were ready. Religious patients told me they were comforted knowing they were going to be with their God.

This is still a very challenging time for loved ones. If the patient has her wits about her, friends and relatives now need to encourage their loved ones—telling them that yes, it is time and that yes, they are ready. If a dying patient in unable to speak, as a hospice nurse I would often show the family how all of the patient's symptoms have been managed, how we can look to the patient's face and see how peaceful she is. This is the time for everyone, including the dying person, to be able to grieve the life she will never have. I have also told people that this is truly the time to celebrate the loved one's legacy. This person's spirit will live on in all the people whose lives she touched.

There are times when a person who is dying needs permission to die. This can come from loved ones, from the self, from a spiritual leader, or even from a stranger.

It is important for family and loved ones to tell the dying person that it is okay to die, that she will be safe, and that even though she will be gone gone, she is loved and will always be in their hearts. This can ease the person out of any guilty feelings for wanting or needing to die.

People who have really worked out issues with family and friends, and most importantly with themselves, can give permission to themselves to go. This is their way of coming to terms with the inevitable and allowing themselves to ease gently out of life. Giving one's self permission is not an easy thing to do—hopefully, the patient feels love around her.

Often people will chose to die alone, not surrounded by loved ones. Freeing one's self to let go, no matter who is around you, is difficult, but often necessary. It will happen with more ease and feel right if you've made peace with the important people in your life.

There are beautiful examples of strangers giving patients permission to die. One is from my experience as a hospice nurse. I gave permission to so many patients, but this one stands out: it was a young man of sixty-three with many complicated disease processes. His wife and three children were in the hospice unit during the admission, and they were very upset. He came to hospice after deciding to stop aggressive treatment. His family wanted him to fight on, but doctors agreed with him. His diseases were taking over, and there wasn't anything that could be done anymore.

When I was admitting him, I saw and felt his struggle and his family's distress. His wife and children were very angry that they didn't have a private room. Watching his family made the patient upset. When I finished the admission, I went back into the room and told him quietly that I would ask the doctor to prescribe the appropriate medications for his pain and his anxiety. I told him we could also help him with his labored breathing and that we would keep him very comfortable—and I warned him that he might get sleepy. This comforted him.

After the medication took effect, it was easy to see how much more at peace he felt. There was not a sound in the room. His wife and children sat on his bed. I took his hand in mine, and I looked into his eyes and told him once again that we would keep him as comfortable as possible. He looked at me and asked if he started to die, would we stop him? I told him the truth. I said no, we will let you die peacefully. Even I started to cry because it seemed to be what he wanted. This was a very special and intense moment for all of us—his children and wife heard, saw, and felt it. They understood. He was getting permission from me to let go and die. It felt as if he and I had been alone in the tiny space, and yet we were surrounded by the enormous love of his wife and children.

This was an honor for me and an enormous relief and gift to this man and his family. I knew he would die soon and peacefully. He died the next day.

Not everyone has such a beautiful experience—but the people that learn that this is possible will know what a gift it is. It unburdens everyone, and death comes with less struggle.

In my years as a hospice nurse, I have found that the most important permission comes from the family. Once again, family and loved ones must realize the need to separate from their own grief in order to let someone go. We must always think of the patient first and not our needs. As a hospice nurse, I have so often seen people who cannot give this permission, who cannot allow the patient to take sufficient pain medications. Without acceptance and proper medication, death becomes a very slow and painful process—difficult to watch, most of all for the patient. There have been so many times I've had to say, "This is not about you."

I see and feel the pain that loved ones go through, but the biggest burden is for the person who is dying. If families and friends can face the reality and accept the inevitable, their loved ones can suffer less. At the end of life, our job is to help people celebrate their life *and* their death.

One Saturday, there was a Jewish family visiting their loved one at the care center. She was actively dying, and they very much wanted a rabbi to be with her before she died. They felt she really would have wanted this. I got on the phone and spent about an hour or so calling every rabbi in the area. None were available. It was the Jewish Sabbath. Our center's rabbi was on vacation, but I knew his cell phone number. I figured most rabbis wouldn't answer a phone on Saturday, but I gave it a shot. The rabbi saw the hospice-center telephone number appear and must have known it was urgent. He answered, and I explained the family's dilemma. He offered to pray with the patient by telephone, so I explained this to the family, and they agreed. Although this woman was no longer conscious, I explained to the family that hearing was the last sense to go when a patient is dying.

I put the telephone to her ear while the rabbi spoke to her and sang a beautiful prayer in Hebrew. We put the phone on speaker, and as the rabbi sang the last words of the prayer, this woman passed gently. I told the rabbi what had happened. He was so pleased to take part in helping the woman slip away peacefully.

This particular woman was an observant Jew, but I've found that often even people who are not at all religious find great comfort in speaking with a rabbi or pastor. A patient's love, kindness, and forgiving nature come through when they come in contact with a spiritual person.

I have never been near death in my own lifetime, but I have witnessed countless deaths, and it is absolutely true that the moment of death is peaceful. The face shows relief, losing any look of pain. I have found this to be comforting. I've been with many families during a patient's "last breath" and have witnessed that they, too, are very comforted. This peacefulness is their last memory—a good one.

After the death of a loved one, everyone grieves in her own way. There is help for those who have an extremely difficult time. There are grievance counselors; grievance groups (offered by hospice centers and others), spiritual and religious leaders, social workers and psychologists. Death often brings families closer. Especially when it comes with acceptance.

Notes:

Agencies

International Cemetery, Cremation and Funeral Association

www.iccfa.com

(800) 645-7700

National Funeral Directors Association

www.nfda.org

(800) 228-6332

U.S. Department of Veterans Affairs

   National Cemetery Administration

   www.cem.va.gov

   (800) 827-1000

Social Security Administration

   www.ssa.gov

   (800) 772-1213 or (TTY) 800-325-0778

National Hospice and Palliative Care

Organization

   www.nhpco.org

   (703) 837-1500

American Cancer Society

   www.cancer.org

   (800) 227-2345

Alzheimer's foundation of America

http://alzfdn.org

Health Care Advocates:

Each state has its own organization.

Each state has its own listings for hospice and palliative Care organizations.

About the Author:

Born in New York, Cynthia Casoff Henry worked as a nurse midwife for many years. For the past eight and a half years, Cynthia has been a hospice nurse. At present, she is traveling the USA in her RV with her husband and a dog and cat.

Made in the USA
Lexington, KY
08 June 2013